THE CROMFORD GUIDE

Freda Bayles
&
Janet Ede

SCARTHIN BOOKS

CONTENTS

Facing page: Leawood Pump House.

—————— **ACKNOWLEDGEMENTS** ——————

We should like to thank the Cromford people who have talked and shared memories with us, and everyone who has contributed information.
Special thanks are due to Darrell Clark, Barry Joyce and Angus Watson for their helpful comments on the manuscript. Thanks go to Kim who walked everywhere with us and to Pamela Hopkinson, editor.

The Cromford Guide

Design and maps: Ivan Sendall

Phototypesetting and printing by Mercia Image, Derby

Published 1994 by Scarthin Books, Cromford, Derbyshire

© Freda Bayles and Janet Ede

ISBN 0907 758 76 2

These walks have been planned to show something of Cromford and its immediate surroundings and to give an indication of life in the village today.

The old name Crumforde appears in the Domesday Survey as a small leadmining hamlet and refers to a ford at a bend in the road or river. The area is rich in a wide range of minerals and rocks. Quarrying for limestone has played an important part in the life of the area, and the high vantage points of Walk 3 give marvellous panoramic views of the quarries, some worked out and some still providing jobs for local people.

The Romans were drawn to the area by the opportunities for easily accessible lead, a valuable commodity used for roofing, baths and gutters, and since the 17th century as a constituent in paint. The lost Roman town of Lutudarum was situated somewhere in the area, possibly at Wirksworth, once the second most populous town in the county. Pigs (ingots) of lead have been found stamped with the name *Lutudarum*. At Carsington where there is a new reservoir, opened in 1992, a villa site has been located.

Scarthin early this century.

The River Derwent flows beside Cromford village, and water, which Derbyshire has in abundance, has been a key factor in the development of its industrial life and tourist industry. Water power was one of the main magnets which drew Richard Arkwright to the area in the eighteenth century, when large scale cotton spinning developed. The industrial village of Cromford and the mill area built by Arkwright are covered in Walks 1 and 2.

An invaluable picture of the village in the late nineteenth century is given in many of the books written by Alison Uttley. She lived at Castle Top Farm, overlooking the Lea road, and described in detail her visits to Cromford and the surrounding villages in her father's pony and trap.

Her accounts have been collected in *Our Village; Alison Uttley's Cromford* (Scarthin Books) which provides a vivid accompaniment to the picture of Cromford as it is seen on the three walks. She brings to life the picture of a small rural community when the heyday of its industrial life was over.

Included in that book is a plan of the village as it was in her childhood, with identification of some of the shops and buildings, some of whose use remains unchanged today.

Willersley Castle, the home Arkwright built but never lived in.

For the best understanding of the history and development of Cromford, follow the walks in the order given. Walks 1 and 2 around the village are very short and are mostly on pavements. Walk 3 includes a stretch of canal towpath, approximately one mile long, and a 4-mile stretch of the High Peak Trail which includes two steep inclines. The towpath and trail can be muddy in places and you will need good walking shoes or boots.

Travelling to Cromford

Cromford lies $2\frac{1}{2}$ miles from Matlock and 18 miles from Derby on the A6. It can be reached by train from Derby, Belper or Matlock; or by bus from Chesterfield, Manchester, Buxton, Nottingham and Derby. For timetable details, see the Useful Telephone Numbers on page 8.

The Yard at Arkwright's Mill.

Car parking in Cromford

Car parking may be difficult in the village itself, but there are plenty of spaces available at Cromford Wharf and at the Arkwright's Mill complex for visitors to that site.

Traffic

Cromford is bisected by roads carrying heavy traffic. The A6 in particular is very busy and should be crossed with extreme care using the pelican crossing shown on the map on page 22.

Wheelchair Access

Walk 1 Suitable for wheelchairs up to (3) and from (9) to (16). Omit Cromford bridge area and Cromford station because of slopes and lack of footpaths.

Walk 2 Cromford Market Place is suitable, but there are slopes and uneven pavements which could be difficult on the remainder of the walk.

Walk 3 Cromford Wharf area and the towpath are possible as far as the Leawood Arm (6), though the towpath can be muddy at times. If you drive to Black Rocks (17) and Middleton Top (18) there are car parks and picnic areas at the Information Centres, and flat stretches along the High Peak Trail at both points. From Middleton Top there is access to about a mile of flat trail in the northern direction. This is a very pleasant walk in open countryside with wonderful elevated views and abundant wild flowers.

Toilets with wheelchair access marked on maps where possible. Also available at Black Rocks Information Centre (upper car park), and Middleton Top Information Centre.

Useful Telephone Numbers

Arkwright's Mill	0629 824297
Derbyshire Dales District Council, Tourism Officer	0629 580580
Cycle Hire, Middleton Top	0629 823204
Ranger Service, Middleton Top & High Peak Junction	0629 823204
	& 0629 822831

British Rail	0332 257000
Trent Busline	0332 292200

Tourist Information Centre, Matlock Bath   0629 55082

Leawood Pumphouse - details of firing times can be obtained from Middleton Top and High Peak Junction Information Centres.

Further Information

Reference materials on the area and its history can be obtained from:

Matlock Library, Steep Turnpike, Matlock   0629 582480
small local history collection.

Derbyshire Record Office

Ernest Bailey Buildings, New St, Matlock   0629 580000 Ext. 7347
The county collection of archive material and maps. It is advisable to ring beforehand to check opening times and availability of materials.

Local Studies Library

County Offices, Bank Road, Matlock   0629 580000 Ext. 6597
An extensive collection of printed materials, St Catherines's House Index, old newspapers, census records.

Workers' houses in North Street.

Mill Road, with the great wall of Arkwright's Mill on the right, and
above the road, the cast iron aqueduct which carried water to the Mill.

approximately 1 mile
map at centre pages

START at Arkwright's Mill in Cromford. The mill is signed off the A6 at the Cromford - Wirksworth crossroads in the Crich direction.

Park in the mill car park and go through the fortress-like gates into the mill complex which has toilets, a cafe, shops and offices. There are excellent guide boards sited around the mill and yard plus a slide/tape sequence and exhibition room. Various books, leaflets and tours are available, therefore what follows is an introductory outline only.

1 Richard Arkwright was born in Preston, Lancashire, in 1732, the thirteenth child of a tailor. As a young man he worked as a barber and wigmaker. He met John Kay, a clockmaker from Warrington, who encouraged him to design a machine to make cotton into a fine strong thread for the warp. This was to revolutionise the cotton industry.

In 1768 he moved to Nottingham and built a small factory where machinery was driven by horsepower. In 1771 he came to Cromford where there was unlimited water power and security from mill-wreckers, workers threatened with loss of livelihood as mass manufacturing began to oust cottage industry. The key to his success came in 1771 when, with several partners, he signed a lease for the water rights of Cromford Sough and Bonsall Brook.

A sough is a tunnel constructed to drain surplus water away from the lead mines. Being underground, soughs do not freeze in winter, a useful factor in maintaining water power.

In Cromford he transformed what had been a small farming and leadmining community into a "crowded village with cottages, supported by three magnificent cotton mills. There is so much water, so much rock, so much population and so much wood that it looks like a Chinese town." (J. Byng, contemporary writer).

The mill complex, near the site of an old lead smelting works, developed from the first building in 1771 and proved a highly prosperous concern. By 1840 the cotton business was curtailed when Meerbrook Sough, dug to provide deeper drainage, depleted the water supply to Arkwright's Mill. Arkwright's machinery, by then very old fashioned, could not easily be adapted to steam power; the buildings were then used for paint grinding and brewing.

The mills formed the model for factories all over the world, notably the Ratingen mill, built in 1783, the first water-powered spinning in Europe, and called Cromford after their English originator. The workers' houses on North Street were the precursor of the great industrial complexes of the next century, for example Saltaire in Yorkshire.

2 Go out of the main mill gate and turn left along the road to St Mary's Church. The church building was begun by Sir Richard Arkwright in 1786 as a private family chapel and completed by his son, also Richard, in 1797. It was later to be used by local people.
Originally this was a plain Georgian building with a simple front and two rows of windows down each side. It was extensively renovated in the 1850s by Peter Arkwright. The two rows of side windows were knocked into one and the arches were pointed in the Gothic style. An imposing porch was added and the tower enlarged and decorated with corner turrets.

Inside, mural paintings by A.O. Hemming were added in 1897, together with stained glass windows behind the altar, to celebrate the centenary. The gallery and organ, thought to date from 1797 to 1801, are unusual features in a small rural church. Amongst many monuments, the most outstanding is an alabaster family group by Sir Francis Chantrey, a nineteenth century Derbyshire sculptor.

Arkwright family tombs can be seen in the churchyard by the river. From here there is an excellent view of Cromford Bridge. Stonework under the arches provides evidence of the existence of an older, narrower, packhorse bridge, widened about 1700.

The church is only open at service times (see notice board).

3 From the churchyard Willersley Castle can be seen standing high across the river. Richard Arkwright began to build it in 1786 on land bought from Thomas Hallet Hodges. Like many self-made men, he wished to emulate the great landed estates of the pre-industrial era. William Thomas, a London architect, was employed for the design and building. It was nearing completion when damaged by fire in 1791 and so was not lived in by Arkwright who died in 1792. It is now a Methodist hotel and conference centre.

4 Turn left outside the churchyard and walk to Cromford Bridge. This fifteenth century millstone grit structure stands on the site of an ancient ford. Notice that the arches on the upstream side, which take the full rush of the current, are rounded, built when the bridge was widened, while the pointed Gothic arches are earlier. On the parapet near the black and white road chevrons is a crude inscription:

THE LEAP OF MR B H MARE JUNE 1697

This commemorates a feat of horsemanship, when Mr. Benjamin Haywood's mare took fright and jumped over the parapet, miraculously bearing her rider to safety.

Cromford Bridge, eastern elevation.

5 Two interesting structures stand at the side of the bridge: an eighteenth century fishing temple, and the remains of a fifteenth century bridge chapel. Both can be seen from the bridge, or more easily by going through the gate into Cromford Meadows and turning left. The fishing temple, inscribed *Piscatoribus Sacrum*, restored in 1968, is a replica of the one in Beresford Dale used by Charles Cotton and Isaac Walton.

6 The foundations and walls are all that remain of the bridge chapel, which served as a place of worship for travellers. High up in the wall overlooking the river is a small, round squint window. Here a lamp would have been placed as a guiding light to people journeying.

Chapel ruins beside the river.

7 Walk over the bridge and past the entrance of Willersley Castle to Bridge House. The steep road to Starkholmes on the left was once part of the ancient road to Matlock before the A6 was blasted through to Matlock Bath in the 1820s.

Bridge House, one of the oldest in Cromford, shows traces of a sixteenth century doorhead and mullioned windows.

8 Continue along the Lea/Crich road for 250 yards and take a left turn before the railway bridge to Cromford Station. The railway, part of the route to Manchester, reached here in 1849.

Alison Uttley describes the charm of this little station from which she set out to school each day. "At our station there were only wild flowers, but there was the compensation of the station buildings with their turrets, wooden spires and white-painted railings." She says that the then Duke of Devonshire took Joseph Paxton, the garden designer and architect, to the site. He suggested a station house built like a French or Swiss chalet, in keeping with the landscape. It was Paxton's son-in-law, G.H. Stokes, who designed and built the station. Castle Top Farm, where Alison Uttley lived, stands on the hillside further along the valley.

Cromford station.

9 Retrace your steps over the bridge to the canal wharf opposite the mill car park. Before the development of the road, now the A6, in the 1820s and the railway in the 1840s, movement of goods in and out of the Cromford area was slow. It was this which motivated influential local people including Arkwright, Outram, the Gells and Hodgkinsons to set up a company with shares at £100 each for the development of Cromford Canal.

The 1789 Act of Parliament authorising this mentioned specifically the transport of coal, limestone, lead, stone, timber, alabaster, marble, textiles and cotton fibres. Contemporary posters show that passengers were also regularly carried on fast "fly" boats. The canal, built by William Jessop, and Benjamin Outram at a cost of £80,000, was opened in late 1793 and ran $14\frac{1}{2}$ miles, from Cromford to Langley Mill. Here it linked with the Erewash Canal, opened 1779, which ran into the River Trent. This provided access to Nottingham and Derby and from there to Liverpool and Manchester via the Trent and Mersey Canal.

The builders of the canal were able to use the water leaving Arkwright's Mill. This proved inadequate when a lead mining sough was constructed, diverting the water, and a pumping engine had to be installed at Leawood (see page 38) to raise water from the Derwent. Despite difficulties which meant that the canal could only be worked north of Butterley Tunnel by narrow boats of 7 foot beam, it proved very profitable.

By the 1850s the Midland Railway to Manchester via Buxton had taken much of the traffic, and after years of decline the canal was abandoned as a commercial waterway in 1944.

Walk 3 begins at the wharf and takes the visitor along the towpath to the High Peak Junction.

10 Leave the wharf by turning left onto Mill Road. Situated high upon the cliff is Rock House, Arkwright's home, from where he could look out of his windows and see all the activity of the mill below. He was to die here in 1792. The path up to Scarthin Rock (16) gives an excellent view of the house and its elevated position.

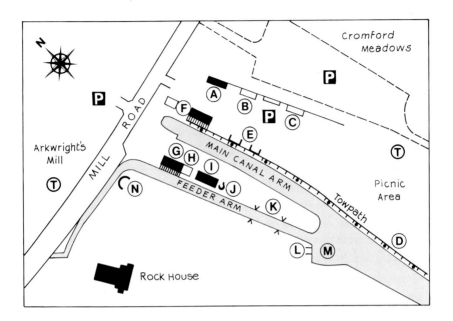

A   Cottages, c1796.

B   Site of smith and stabling.

C   Site of sawpit.

D   Rings along towpath for tying up boats.

E   Cart loading bays, raised for easy loading.

F   Warehouse, c1824, covered loading bay and weighbridge.

G   Counting house 1794, with slate-covered loading bay, where tonnage and rates paid.

H   Stabling for horses, notice manger.

I   First warehouse, c1794, upper doors for loading high carts.

J   Simple crane attached to building.

K   Slots for stop planks to isolate feeder arm for boat repairs.

L   Entrance to Arkwright's boathouse.

M   'Winding' hole, where boats of 60 feet could be turned.

N   Archway, possibly from Rock House.

P   Car Park

T   Toilets

11 This was the Mill Manager's house, well-situated to allow overseeing of the site. A driveway at the side leads up to Rock House, and the small alleyway led to Intake Lane and gave easy access to the village for mill workers.

12 Continue along the main road. Notice above you a cast iron aqueduct, dated 1821, which carried water to drive the overshot millwheel. Originally there would have been a wooden aqueduct.

13 On your right is an opening leading to further mill buildings. The building with the decorated wooden cornice at roof level, built c.1783 to 86, is thought to have been a counting house, where goods were checked in and out of the mill. Grace Cottage, originally redbrick but now rendered, matches the Counting House identically in style under its rendering. It is thought to have been the gatekeeper's cottage.

Artist's impression of the Derby Road at Scarthin Nick, early 20th century.

14 Walk towards the main road and turn right. The small polygonal cafe on the A6 was once a barber's shop. Alison Uttley describes it "alone in its glory, crouched at the foot of the cliff" with its long barber's pole striped in red and white projecting from the front. The windows were filled with tobacco twists, jars of sweets, cigarettes and long pipes. Customers sat on the wooden benches round the walls and gossiped while waiting their turn.

15 Towering above the barber's shop is the massive cliff face of Scarthin. This was originally a continuous rock formation across the road separating Matlock Bath from Cromford. In 1771 the deeds for Arkwright's lease of Cromford land mention an "intended cut" through the rock face. A narrow passageway was blasted through in the early 1790s.

In 1817 a Turnpike Act empowered the building of a road. This

Arkwright's Masson Mill.

was constructed by Smith and Pennell, who had enlarged the Old Bath Hotel at Matlock Bath where visitors came to take the spa waters. Easy access to Matlock Bath and the Peak District became important as the area developed as a fashionable watering place. The road was further widened in 1961 to 62.

16 Go forward to the gateway on the right and continue down the track by the river. This private carriageway, built by Arkwright beside the Derwent, gave him easy access to Willersley and Masson Mill. It probably follows the line of an old track running under the cliff face.

At the end of this path take the wooden steps on the right behind the car park leading up to Scarthin Rock. This path gives a magnificent view of Willersley Castle and the surrounding countryside, but walkers should note that it is steep, and although fenced, the drop is precipitous. The rock used to be known locally as Violet Rock, after the scented white violets that abounded there in spring.

17 The tall red chimney of Masson Mill can be seen across the Derwent. The central portion, with its semi-circular Venetian windows, was built by Arkwright in 1783 to 84.

Its redbrick structure is in marked contrast to the rough-hewn, fortress-like appearance of Arkwright's Mill.

Return down the steps to the Mill complex and car park.

A barge horse at the canal wharf.
Facing page: Bridge over canal - note grooving
in stonework caused by tow ropes.

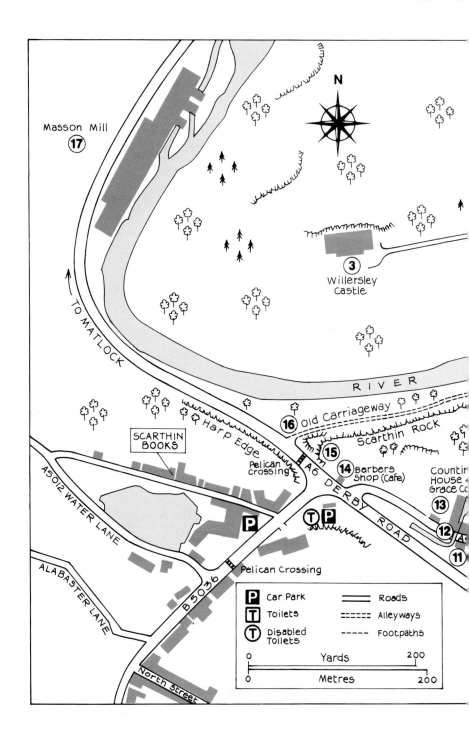

Masson Mill
17

N

TO MATLOCK

3
Willersley
Castle

R I V E R

16 Old Carriageway

SCARTHIN
BOOKS

Harp Edge

Scarthin Rock

Pelican
crossing

15

A6

14 Barbers
Shop (Cafe)

Countir
House
Grace Co

13

A5012 WATER LANE

DERBY

ROAD

12

11

ALABASTER LANE

P

T P

B5036

Pelican Crossing

P	Car Park		Roads
T	Toilets		Alleyways
T	Disabled Toilets		Footpaths

0   Yards   200
0   Metres   200

North Street

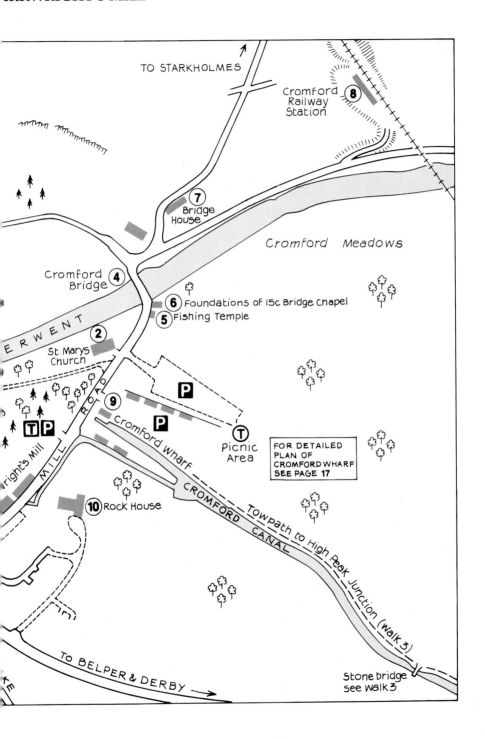

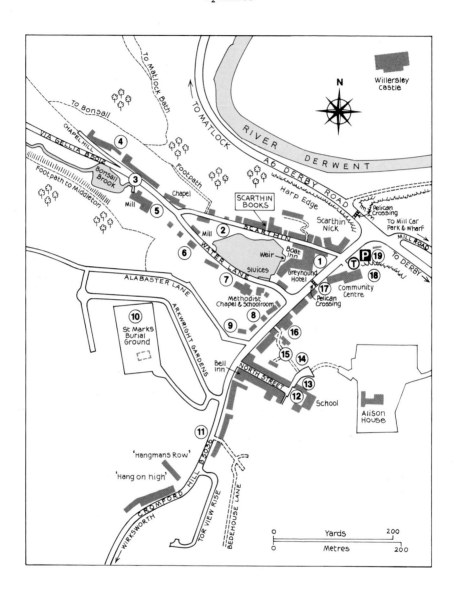

START in Cromford market place.

Parking in the market place is limited. Use the Mill car park or Cromford Wharf and walk back the 250 yards to the village. There are also parking spaces past the Community Centre behind the public toilets.

1 Before Arkwright came to Cromford, it was a small agricultural and leadmining community. However, the influx of workers to the mill created a need for shops, and Arkwright built these round the market place. A Charter was granted for a market, held each Saturday until 1880. The Greyhound Inn was built in 1778 for businessmen and as a staging post, connecting with London, Manchester and Birmingham. The houses next to the Greyhound, with their low display windows, were originally shops.

Beneath the market place run a series of well-constructed water courses, carrying the Bonsall Brook from behind the Inn under the road to the mill. The small bridge by the War Memorial (19) spans this brook.

Our Village by Alison Uttley (see page 6) contains a map of the village as she remembered it from the 1890s. A wide range of shops served her community. On the corner and up the flight of steps was a tailor's shop; the present restaurant was a bootmakers; next door was a chemist as it is today.

2 Walk up the narrow, one-way lane called Scarthin. The closely-packed cottages on the right are all that remain of the small seventeenth and eighteenth century leadminers' settlement of Scarthin, built on the steep sides of the hill.

The Boat Inn (formerly the Bull's Head), built in 1772, indicates the growing population and wealth of this new industrial village. Behind the pub and below the railings are the remains of wooden shuttering which controlled the water flow from the pond to the water courses running under the market place.

Three chapel buildings remain in Scarthin; one converted to a workshop, another to a house, and a third to a garage. These indicate the strength and variety of Non-Conformism in the area.

Beside the workshop, Chapel Steps ran up to an older meeting place called the Long Room, later incorporated into a chapel built in 1868 by A. Wyatt: "In the midst of the poor and exclusively for their use." The present chapel was built around 1912.

Bakehouse Cottages on the right are built on the site of an old bakehouse.

Opposite the Primitive Methodist Chapel, 1853, a worn flag path or "pitchings" runs up by the side of a house. This is the beginning of public footpaths leading to Matlock Bath and the old leadmining village of Bonsall, which make delightful and spectacular walks.

Cromford Market Place.

3 Turn right out of Scarthin into the Via Gellia. This road is not, as the name suggests, Roman, but was built by the Gell family of Hopton, local landowners. It was originally a track built about 1791 to carry lead and other minerals from the hillside to the canal. In 1804 it became a turnpike road.

Continue past the hairdresser and the motor workshop housed in a former chapel building. In the 1920s the shop next door sold music and was used for slide shows. This area of industrial housing, possibly earlier than North Street (12), is known as Staffordshire Row, because originally workers had been brought from Staffordshire and housed there.

4 Walk up Chapel Hill, which rises above the main road.
While the redbrick Swiss Cottage at the bottom of Chapel Hill is
of a more recent date, the imposing stone terrace at the top is
clearly much older. Number 16, Via Gellia House with its large
bays, was built by Nathaniel Wheatcroft about 1780 and originally included Number 18. The Wheatcroft family operated
boats on the canal wharf and in 1830 advertised fast passenger
boats; the house was occupied by the family until well into the
nineteenth century, and the name can still be seen on the wharf.

Number 22 with its fine porch was built about 1780 although
interior evidence of roof lines and windows suggests it may
incorporate an older building.

Number 26 still has original cast iron window frames in the
upper storey, with small inner lights.

At the rear, the houses have doors in the first storey which
may well have been used for unloading outwork from the mills.
At one time a track ran up behind the terrace from where Swiss
Cottage now stands. The track at the end leads to the village of
Bonsall.

As you return down the terrace, notice the blue gabled house
above Number 6 which was at one time a training college for
the Methodist Ministry.

Chapel Hill provides an excellent view of the dammed Bonsall
Brook, on the opposite side of the road, and the sluices which
channelled water to the adjacent mill, powered by the brook.

The old leadmining settlement of Scarthin.

5 Cross the Via Gellia to the mill. Probably built by Richard Arkwright about 1780, it ground flour for the parish and ceased working in 1935. The gate in the wall provides access but care is needed as the water channel is fast flowing. The recess and shaft for the wooden wheel can be seen.

The footpath below the yard entrance leads up the hillside towards Rose End Meadows Nature Reserve and to paths along the Via Gellia and the village of Middleton.

The overshot waterwheel.

6 Return to the village past the garage and small row of industrial housing. On the opposite side of the road is another mill, now a cane workshop, but formerly a paint grinding mill. Here a very fine mid-nineteenth century waterwheel survives, driven by water originally carried in two overhead iron pipes from the cornmill opposite, controlled by the wooden sluice gates near the road.

7 Continue past the Methodist Chapel. The chapel and schoolroom were completed in 1900 and continue to thrive. In the corner of the pond beside the motor workshop are the remains of one of the sluices which controlled the water flow.

8 Continue to the main road and turn right up the hill. Opposite the butcher's shop is a curious round stone let into the wall which was a stand for buckets when the houses relied on an outside water supply.

Bucket stand.

Further up the hill is a Working Men's Institute, built by Peter Arkwright for the men of the village. It provided a reading room and meeting place and was a symbol of the Victorian belief in self-education. It is now the venue for village meetings of all kinds.

An old cottage in Alabaster Lane.

9 Continue up the hill to Alabaster Lane. The house on the corner with its small mullioned windows is one of the oldest in the village pre-dating Arkwright. Alabaster Lane may be so-called because it marked a path where alabaster, a smooth white soft limestone, widely used for church monuments and interiors of buildings, was brought down from the hillside. A sough known as Alabaster Sough feeds into the Greyhound pond at Cromford.

10 Walk on up the hill and turn right into Arkwright Gardens, bearing left towards St Mark's Cemetery. As St Mary's Church did not possess a public burial ground funerals had to take place in Wirksworth. In 1877 a piece of land was provided by the Arkwright family, and a small church, St Mark's, built there. This fell into disuse and was demolished in 1971.

11 Return to the main road and continue up the hill. The road runs on the site of a medieval trackway. The steep ascent to Wirksworth is constantly busy with traffic today.

Looking down North Street towards Cromford Hill.

The houses on either side are of interest; many were built by Arkwright and his family for their workers, although they are of a later date than North Street (12). Look for the oldest windows, metal-framed with an inner opening light. At one time a gulley for drainage ran down the west side of the hill and the local "marble" bridges which gave access to the houses could be seen.

Numbers 95 and 97 have had their fronts restored as closely as possible to the originals, under the Cromford Town Scheme. This grant scheme has generated a number of large and small restoration projects since its inception in 1987. Notice the round-headed windows and the fine stonework.

Directly opposite Tor View Rise is a row of cottages locally known as "Hangman's Row". The hill behind is known as "Hang on High".

12 Cross over the road and return downhill, turning into North Street. The Bell Inn (formerly The Blue Bell) is on one corner; opposite is a bay-windowed house, once the Cock Inn.

Almost a model village in one lane, North Street was a complete Arkwright creation, built between 1776 and 1777 to house mill workers. The attic storey of each dwelling had a range of windows to give good light for the outworkers at their frames.

The cottages were very well built for the period, with outside sanitation and most had a strip of garden at the rear. Some are

Cromford School.

The walls of the 'Bear Pit' sluice.

now holiday cottages and Number 10 on the left at the far end is owned by the Landmark Trust and rented out for holiday accommodation. It has been internally restored and furnished in keeping with the period. A feature of this and others in the street is that their roofing is of nail-less Staffordshire blue tiles, although to the rear some 18th century red clay tiles survive.

Arkwright began a Sunday School in Cromford in the 1770s and later, in 1832, his only son, Richard Arkwright founded the school at the end of the street, with provision for 200 girls and boys, and a house at the side for the schoolmaster.

13 Turn left by the Landmark Trust cottage and then take the left-hand path through a gap in the wall. Various stone-built pig sties and troughs can be seen in the allotments. People relied on home-fed pig products for much of their food. Arkwright was a skillful manager of men, and a shrewd as well as benevolent employer, operating a system of gifts and rewards as incentives for his workers.

14 Continue on this path as it bears round to the left. Situated in the yard is the old village lock-up, now owned by the Arkwright Society. Inside are two small cells where offenders were detained before being taken elsewhere for trial.

15 Retrace your steps to the magnificent circular sluice. It is locally known as the Bear Pit.

The sluice was a collection point for water draining from lead mines at Black Rocks and a means of topping up the Greyhound pond. Work began on this structure about 1672 with the intention of draining Gang Vein Mine, in the Black Rocks area, but ventilation problems delayed completion of the mile-long tunnel until 1709. Richard Arkwright bought the rights to this sough and used the water power to drive machinery at his mills. Water flow was controlled by the sluice gates and wooden stop boards.

Looking down into the sluice.

16 Walk on past the sluice through a passageway between houses and turn right down the hill. Part of the Arkwright Stores was a Post Office for many years. Note the bow-fronted window frames.

17 A few yards further on is the Blacksmith's shop. As its name suggests, this was the village smithy, a working forge for nearly 200 years until the 1950s. Some of the original windows are unchanged, and the forge entrance is now closed by large wooden doors. The present owner took over from his father in the 1920s thus continuing a long family association.

  Alison Uttley gives a vivid picture of work being done there, with two or three horses waiting to be shod by the blacksmith wearing his leather apron, his face and hair black, blowing the fire with wheezing bellows, and producing showers of sparks as he shaped the horseshoes on the anvil.

18 Walk on the attractive footpath of stone sets past the bakery to the Community Centre, formerly a flour mill.

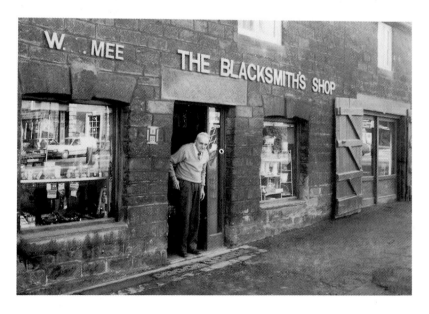

Mr Mee in the doorway of the blacksmiths's shop.

19 The Memorial Gardens commemorate the sacrifices of two World Wars. A goit carrying water from the leadmine, which was used by Arkwright to power his first mill, is spanned by the remains of a very old bridge behind the wall, best seen from the A6 roadside.

Return to the car park.

Stone water trough at the end of North Street.

6 $\frac{1}{4}$ Miles   **Shorter Variation 2 Miles**

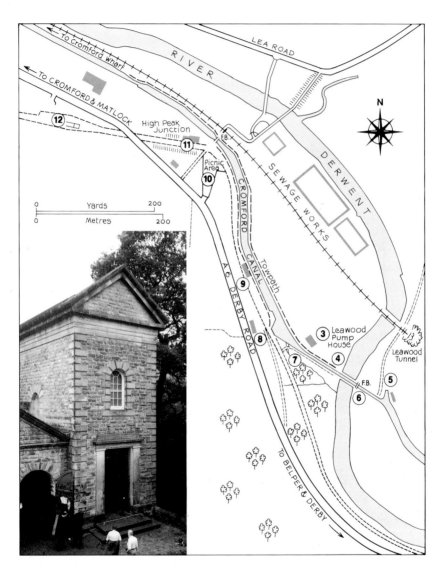

Members of the Middleton Engine Group running the pump at
Leawood Pump House.

START at Cromford Wharf. Park on the Wharf car park. The
wharf area is described in Walk 1, page 16.

1 Walk along the canal towpath as far as the stone bridge (shown on map 1, page 22-23). This may have been built for the passage of animals from the moorland to the meadows. Note the grooves on the sides of the tunnel and above the path; these have been worn by ropes rubbing as a horse pulled the barge along.

Further on, water can be seen draining into the canal from its far bank. This is a drainage tunnel, one of many constructed, mainly during the seventeenth century, to drain surplus water away from the lead mines.

2 Cromford Canal was cut through the ancient woods of Crich Chase, and there is a rich legacy of wildlife throughout its length. Even in winter there is abundant bird and plant life; some 250 species of the latter have been noted during the seasons. Insects abound, particularly butterflies, and the water is home to a variety of fish, and to water voles.

High Peak Junction workshops.

3 Pass High Peak Junction on the opposite bank, but stay on the left bank to reach Leawood Pump House. In 1825 the subscribers, including Richard Arkwright (junior) and the Duke of Devonshire, secured an Act of Parliament for the building of a railway link, and the line was partially opened in 1830 and finally completed to Whaley Bridge in July 1831.

 Just before the Pump House is the entry point for water raised from the river, which is controlled by stop planks.

 Built in 1849, Leawood Pump House contains the great beam engine and pump used to raise water 30ft up from the Derwent and replenish the canal during times of drought or shortage. It has been restored and can at intervals be seen in steam and working. Dates and times for steaming are available from Middleton Top or High Peak Junction Centres, telephone numbers page 8.

4 The Wigwell Aqueduct was built in 1793 by William Jessop to carry the canal over the River Derwent. When serious cracks began to show within months of completion Jessop accepted full responsibility and had all necessary rebuilding done at his own expense. Look over the aqueduct parapet where you will see the arched tunnel where water was drawn from the river and raised 30 feet to feed into the canal.

5 Leawood Branch, or Nightingale Arm, joins the canal at the south end of the aqueduct, and was made in 1802 to carry textiles down from Lea Mills, and lead from a smelting works near Lea village.

6 Cross the canal by a wooden bridge; retrace your route on the opposite bank. Below is another stop plank, to control the water level.

7 It is worth turning left here to go down the path to the river bank. Now one can see and appreciate the fine architecture of Jessop's construction, an 80 foot span, three-arched bridge. The date plaque is still visible.

8 Walk to High Peak Junction, following the path along the west bank of the canal. At the north end of the aqueduct is a weir and sluice which allows water to leave the canal and be returned to the river.

9 Follow the path behind the wharf buildings to High Peak Junction. High Peak Junction is where the railway met the canal. Originally a canal link with Whaley Bridge in the north of the county had been envisaged, but difficulties of terrain made this impossible and a rail link was built instead. Nine engine houses were planned to provide power to draw trains up the steep inclines. When the mainline railway came to Cromford in 1849 an extension was built to the High Peak railway to link up with the London-Manchester line. Trucks came down onto the wharf to be unloaded straight into barges. The wharf shed is now a youth centre. Look around for various industrial artefacts including a height gauge above the track.

10 The raised picnic area on the left was originally pasture for the working horses. Some evidence of stabling remains behind the clump of trees.

11 The former workshop buildings now house an information centre, small exhibition, shop and toilets. Note the small swing bridge over the canal which carries the public footpath to Lea Bridge.

12 Follow the High Peak Trail up the steep incline and under the A6 road. On the left is an escape pit which provided a safety catchment for runaway rolling stock; a half-buried truck can still be seen here.

13 Continue climbing to the top of the incline. Notice the efforts made to conserve this well-walked track, using wooden sleepers and gulleys for drainage.
  Further up the incline on the right is a small derelict railway building. On the left is a deep hollow with stone blocks, the site of a former engine house.
  After the stretch of low wall on your left, notice the remains of a wooden crane and quarry face over the wall, where stone would have been cut for making and repairing the trail.

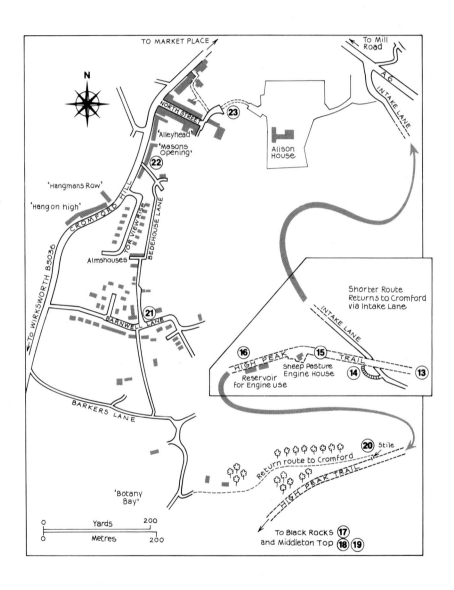

14 To shorten this walk and return to Cromford, take the steps over the wall on the left by the crane (immediately opposite the cyclist warning board on your right). Bear left through the woods, on the track leading through the tunnel and out onto Intake Lane, which gets its name from land enclosure times. Walk down with the housing estate on your right, to the A6. Cross the road and return to the Wharf.

15 Near the top of the incline you pass a magnificent rocky outcrop on the left which serves as a reminder of the engineering effort required to blast a track through large masses of rock. Occasionally, drilled holes in the rock show where charges were inserted for blasting.

Sheep Pasture Engine House is at the top of the incline, a fine old building, still standing impressively although all the machinery has been removed from it. A few yards on, look to the right for a magnificent view, including Dene and Ball Eye Quarries. Quarrying was able to develop in this district because of the nearness of canal and rail facilities.

Cromford is spread like a map in the foreground of this panorama, Matlock Bath in the middle distance, Starkholmes and Riber Castle to the right and Matlock Moor on the skyline.

Black Rocks.

16 Continue on the trail as it levels out. The reservoir on the left supplied water for railway use.

   On the right immediately after open fields at the start of woodland, you will see the broken signpost and narrow stone squeeze stile which is the point where you leave the trail for your return later at (20).

17 (not shown on map) Follow the High Peak Trail through the Black Rocks area. This high gritstone outcrop is popular with locals and visitors alike for its woodland walks, rock climbing and fine panoramic views. Parking, explanatory notice boards, Visitor Centre, picnic tables and toilets are also available on this site.

18 (not shown on map) Continue to follow the Trail to Middleton Top Engine House. Built between 1825-29 the engine house contains the original working beam engine. Here can be seen the winding engine which assisted steam trains up the steep incline.

   A Visitor Centre occupies part of the site, it includes toilets, shop, and exhibitions including an excellent slide/tape sequence on the history of the railway. Car parking is available and bicycles may be hired to explore the rest of the High Peak Trail, which continues for another $15\frac{1}{2}$ miles and links up with the $15\frac{1}{2}$ miles of Tissington Trail.

19 Turn around here and retrace your steps down the Trail and back through the Black Rocks area.

20 Turn left off the Trail to return to Cromford, by the broken signpost and stone squeeze stile set in the wall (noted on your climb up). Another stile on the right goes through fields, but we follow the ancient trackway to our left which hairpins back and descends through woodland and near some very old housing known as Botany Bay, which is thought to have been named after the Australian settlement of the same name. Note the uneven nature of the fields here, due to the spoils from leadmining.

21 Follow the track down, crossing Barkers Lane and into Barnwell Lane, which has some fine old houses, thence into narrow Bedehouse Lane, where the Bede or Almshouses can be seen on the left.

By her Will of 1662 Dame Mary Armyne, Lady of the Manor of Cromford (a title which Richard Arkwright later purchased) left money and land for the building of bede houses for six poor elderly widows and widowers. The buildings have recently been extensively renovated, and are still lived in.

22 Go on to Cromford Hill, turn right and after a few yards right again into North Street. See Walk 2 (12) for a description of North Street.

23 At the end of North Street on the left is a lane leading to a children's playground and to Alison House. Although Georgian in style, the house was probably constructed in the 1850s, and used to be called Oakhill House. For some years it served as the Vicarage, being occupied by the Reverend G.H. Arkwright, a descendent of Sir Richard. It is now a conference centre and guest house. There is no right of way through the grounds and permission for viewing needs to be obtained from the owner.

24 Return to the Market Place (see map on page 24). Walk along North Street to Cromford Hill and walk down to the Market Place.

25 Return to Cromford Wharf car park. Cross the busy A6 at the pelican crossing and turn right. Walk down Mill Road to the Wharf.

Arkwright and the Mills at Cromford (Arkwright Society 1971)

Our Village - Alison Uttley's Cromford (Scarthin Books, 1984)

The Cromford Canal (Cromford Canal Society, 1983)

Brian & Neville Cooper, *Transformation of a Valley* (Scarthin Books, 1983)

A.E. Dodd & E.M. Dodd, *Peakland Roads and Trackways* (Moorland Publishing, 1974)

R.S. Fitton, *The Arkwrights, Spinners of Fortune* (Manchester University Press, 1989)

David Hay, *Packmen, Carriers and Packhorse Roads* (Leicester University Press, 1970)

E.G. Power, *A Textile Community in the Industrial Revolution* 1969

Alison Uttley, *The Country Child* (Faber & Faber, 1931)

Walter Unsworth, *Portrait of the River Derwent* (Robert Hale 1971)

Henry Thorold, *A Shell Guide to Derbyshire* (Faber & Faber, 1972)

LOCAL AND INDUSTRIAL HISTORY TITLES
PUBLISHED BY SCARTHIN BOOKS

OUR VILLAGE - ALISON UTTLEY'S CROMFORD
A collection of essays vividly recalling scenes from the childhood of the
celebrated essayist and children's writer.
72pp Illustrated by C.F. Tunnicliffe   ISBN 0 907758 08 8

TRANSFORMATION OF A VALLEY by Brian and Neville Cooper
The most readable and authoritative guide to the industrial history of the
area.
316pp, maps and 130 photographs.   ISBN 0 907758 17 7

WALLS ACROSS THE VALLEY by Brian Robinson
The story of the building of the Howden and Derwent dams.
256pp, duotone and colour illustrations   ISBN 0 907758 57 6

DERBYSHIRE IN THE CIVIL WAR by BrianStone
157pp illustrated   ISBN 0 907758 58 4

WATERWAYS TO DERBY by Celia M. Swainson
64pp, illustrated   ISBN 0 907758 59 2

HISTORIC FARMHOUSES AROUND DERBY by Barbara Hutton
64pp, illustrated   ISBN 0 907758 48 7